Fact Finders®

WITHDRAWN

MILITARY HEROES

HARLEM

AFRICAN-AMERICAN HEROES OF WORLD WAR I

HELLFIGHTERS

BY JOHN MICKLOS, JR.

CONSULTANT:
RAYMOND L. PUFFER, PHD
HISTORIAN, RETIRED
EDWARDS AIR FORCE BASE HISTORY OFFICE

CAPSTONE PRESS
a capstone imprint

Fact Finders Books are published by Capstone Press,
1710 Roe Crest Drive, North Mankato, Minnesota 56003
www.mycapstone.com

Library of Congress Cataloging-in-Publication Data
Names: Micklos, John, author.
Title: Harlem Hellfighters : African-American heroes of World War I / by John
   Micklos, Jr.
Description: North Mankato, Minnesota : Fact Finders, an imprint of Capstone
   Press, 2017. | Series: Fact finders. Military heroes | Includes
   bibliographical references and index.
Identifiers: LCCN 2016027450|
ISBN 9781515733485 (library binding) |
ISBN 9781515733508 (eBook PDF)
Subjects: LCSH: United States. Army. Infantry Regiment, 369th—Juvenile literature. | World War, 1914–1918—Participation, African American—Juvenile literature. | United States. Army—African American troops—History—20th century—Juvenile literature. | African American soldiers—History—20th century—Juvenile literature. | Harlem (New York, N.Y.)—Biography—Juvenile literature.
Classification: LCC D570.33 369th M53 2017 | DDC 940.4/127308996073—dc23
LC record available at https://lccn.loc.gov/2016027450

Editorial Credits
Editor: Brenda Haugen
Designer: Kristi Carlson
Media Researcher: Ruth Smith
Production Specialist: Tori Abraham

Photo Credits
Alamy: Chronicle, 21, 25, Granger Historical Picture Archive, 27, pf, 22; Capstone Press: 5; Getty Images: Bettmann, 14-15, FPG, 11 Bottom, 26, Interim Archives, 11 Top, ullstein bild, 4, Underwood Archives, 12; Library of Congress: Edrop, Arthur N, 9; Newscom: Everett Collection, 28; Shutterstock: Everett Collection, 7, cover, 8 Top, 8 Bottom, 18; Superstock: Underwood Photo Archives, 17

Primary Source Bibliography
Page 8—History Matters. "Making the World 'Safe for Democracy': Woodrow Wilson Asks for War." http://historymatters.gmu.edu/d/4943/. Retrieved July 21, 2016.
Pages 10, 17, and 19—Sammons, Jeffrey T., and John H. Morrow, Jr. *Harlem's Rattlers and the Great War.* Lawrence, Kan.: University of Kansas Press, 2014.
Page 15—DuBois, W.E.B. "Close Ranks." *The Crisis.* July 1918.
Pages 16, 23, and 24—Harris, Stephen L. *Harlem's Hell Fighters.* Washington, D.C.: Brassey's, Inc., 2003.
Page 26—Jobs, Sebastian. *Welcome Home, Boys! Military Victory Parades in New York City 1899–1946.* New York: Campus Verlag, 2012.
Page 29—Gates, Jr., Henry Louis. "Who Were the Harlem Hellfighters." PBS. www.pbs.org/wnet/african-americans-many-rivers-to-cross/history/who-were-the-harlem-hellfighters/. Retrieved July 21, 2016.

Printed and bound in China.
009943S17

Table of Contents

CHAPTER 1

THE WORLD AT WAR

War raged across Europe from 1914 to 1918. The world's first global conflict, what we know as World War I, claimed the lives of more than 8.5 million soldiers. It changed forever the scope of wars and the way they were fought.

One simple event triggered World War I. On June 28, 1914, Archduke Franz Ferdinand of Austria was **assassinated** by a young Bosnian Serb named Gavrilo Princip.

Franz Ferdinand and his wife, Sophie, visited city hall in Sarajevo, Bosnia and Herzegovina, shortly before the assassination.

Austria-Hungary controlled Bosnia and Herzegovina, but many Bosnians sought independence. They thought killing the archduke might help bring independence. Instead, the killing led to a chain reaction that soon drew dozens of countries into the conflict. Germany and Austria-Hungary were the main combatants on one side. Those two countries and their **allies** were called the Central Powers. On the other side were France, Great Britain, Russia, Italy, and later, the United States. They and the other countries that fought with them were simply called the Allies.

Central Powers ■   Allies ▨

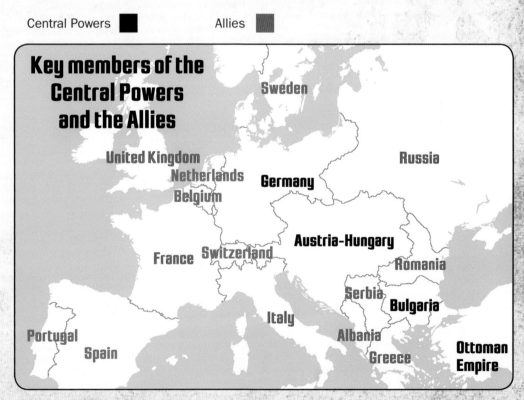

Key members of the Central Powers and the Allies

Sweden

United Kingdom

Russia

Netherlands

Germany

Belgium

France   Switzerland

Austria-Hungary

Romania

Serbia

Bulgaria

Italy

Portugal

Albania

Ottoman Empire

Spain

Greece

assassinate—to murder a person who is well-known or important

allies—people, groups, or countries that work together for a common cause

Germany believed the key to winning the war was to quickly defeat France before Russia could **mobilize** its forces. German leaders hoped to sweep through northern France and capture Paris, the French capital. By early September they were about 30 miles (48 kilometers) from Paris. But at the Battle of the Marne, the French and English armies managed to push the Germans back. By late 1914 both sides had built a series of deep **trenches** along what was called the Western Front.

Strengthened with machine guns and barbed wire, the trenches zigzagged more than 400 miles (644 km) across northern France. For the next three and a half years, the Allies and Central Powers fought a series of bloody battles that cost hundreds of thousands of lives. All this fighting left the basic battle lines little changed.

Because the invasion of France failed, the Central Powers had to fight on two fronts. Fierce battles with Russia raged across eastern Europe for three years. This was called the war's Eastern Front. Then in 1917 a new Communist government took power in Russia. The Russian army had collapsed, and in March 1918, Russia signed a treaty with the Central Powers.

mobilize—get troops and weapons ready for battle

trench—a long, narrow ditch dug in the ground to serve as shelter from enemy fire or attack

German soldiers fired their weapons from trenches during many
World War I battles.

NEUTRAL NO MORE

||||||||||||||||||||||||||||||||||||||||||||||||||

President Woodrow Wilson

At first the United States tried to stay out of the war. U.S. President Woodrow Wilson pledged that the nation would remain **neutral**. It didn't quite manage that. Although not involved in the fighting, the United States provided food and supplies to the Allies. Despite this aid, by 1917 it appeared that without direct U.S. involvement, Germany and Austria-Hungary might win the war.

On April 2, 1917, Wilson asked Congress to declare war on Germany. "The world must be made safe for democracy," he said. On April 6 Congress acted. The United States began massing forces to fight in the Great War. Among those forces was a regiment of African-American soldiers who would fight so fiercely that they would come to be known as the Harlem Hellfighters.

President Woodrow Wilson stood before Congress and asked that the United States join the war.

neutral—not taking sides in a war

A recruitment poster urged men to volunteer for U.S. military service.

CHAPTER 2

FORMING THE 15TH

Even after the United States entered World War I, it seemed highly unlikely that a unit such as the African-American Harlem Hellfighters would ever be involved. In preparation for possible war, many states formed temporary National Guard units. The units were sent to training camps before they were sent overseas. They stood ready to be called into action if needed.

The 15th New York Voluntary Infantry Regiment first formed as a National Guard unit in 1916. New York governor Charles S. Whitman and his legal counsel, William Hayward, both wanted to form an African-American unit in the state. Years earlier, Hayward had been a National Guard colonel in Nebraska. He offered to help organize a regiment in New York. He had one condition. He wanted to lead it. Both Whitman and Hayward were white. They both agreed that "the great colored population of New York ought to be given an opportunity to shine in the National Guard without **prejudice**."

Still, the makeup of the regiment reflected the overall beliefs of the times. The soldiers and some lower-ranking officers were black, but the commanding officers were white. Hayward served as the commanding colonel. The recruits included a professional baseball player, a state legislator, and many general laborers.

The Harlem Hellfighters were among the most highly decorated soldiers of World War I.

Did You Know?

The 15th Regiment adopted the rattlesnake as its symbol, with the words, "Don't tread on me." This symbol had been used by the newly formed United States during the Revolutionary War (1775–1783). In the 1840s noted writer and **abolitionist** Frederick Douglass also compared his former slave master to a snake. In addition, the snake represented African-Americans demanding equality.

prejudice—an opinion about others that is unfair or not based on facts

abolitionist—a person who supported the banning of slavery

EUROPE AND HIS BAND

||||||||||||||||||||||||||||||||||||||||||||||||||||||||||||||||||||||||||||||||

Noted bandleader James Europe joined the unit and agreed to help form a military band. Hayward found a wealthy businessman who agreed to donate $10,000 to buy instruments. The band performed lively jazz music all around New York City. Many recruits joined the guard unit because of the band. By July 1917 the regiment had slightly more than 2,000 men. But the 15th still faced challenges.

Lieutenant James Europe (left) and members of his 369th Infantry Regiment jazz band

A Grand Band

James Reese Europe was a world-renowned bandleader and musician when he was recruited to join the 15th New York National Guard Regiment. Regimental leaders wanted him to form a military band. They thought this might help them attract other recruits. Europe formed a top-notch jazz band. During World War I, the band toured France and Belgium. Their bright, energetic music brought smiles to war-weary listeners. Europe survived the war, but he died soon after. During an argument, a hotheaded band drummer killed him. The noted bandleader died at age 39.

An Unusual Solution

At first the regiment had few rifles. They drilled using broomsticks. When the state delayed providing guns, Hayward found a novel solution. He learned that the state gave rifles to civilian shooting clubs. Members of the regiment began forming such clubs. Soon the regiment had rifles for training.

The United States in 1917 was **segregated**. Across the South, and in many northern areas as well, African-Americans faced severe **discrimination**. They were denied housing in many neighborhoods. They could not enter certain hotels or restaurants. Their children attended separate schools that often were not as good as those that served white children.

As the United States entered World War I, many African-Americans questioned why they should fight for a nation that valued them so little. Others thought having black soldiers might help break racial **stereotypes**. At the time, many whites viewed blacks as inferior. Seeing blacks succeed as soldiers might help change those attitudes.

segregate—to keep groups of people apart, especially based on race

discrimination—unfair treatment of a person or group, often because of race, religion, gender, sexual orientation, or age

stereotype—an overly simple opinion of a person, group, or thing

Segregated drinking fountains were found throughout the South.

One such supporter was noted black professor and activist W.E.B. Du Bois. A founding member of the National Association for the Advancement of Colored People, he often had spoken out against

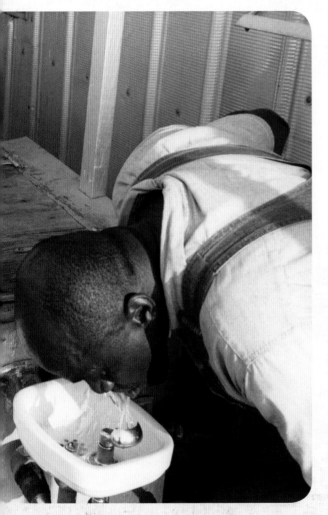

discrimination and racism. But now he called on African-Americans to "forget our special grievances and close our ranks shoulder to shoulder with our white fellow citizens and the allied nations that are fighting for democracy."

Roughly 400,000 African-Americans served in the U.S. armed forces during World War I. Because of discrimination most were assigned noncombat duties behind the lines. Few saw battle action. One group that did was the 15th. The heroic actions of the 15th changed the way many people in the United States viewed African-American soldiers.

CHAPTER 3

FIGHTING FOR EQUALITY

Before they could battle the Germans in France, the men of the 15th had to battle prejudice at home. When they reached training camp in Spartanburg, South Carolina, their presence nearly caused a **race riot**. The first shots of the Civil War (1861–1865) had been fired in South Carolina.

More than 50 years later, prejudice against African-Americans remained strong. Mayor J.F. Floyd of Spartanburg objected to the 15th regiment coming to town. "They will probably expected to be treated like white men," he said. Floyd and other town leaders made it clear that the soldiers would not receive equal treatment.

"If any of those colored soldiers go in any of our soda stores and the like and ask to be served they'll be knocked down."

—a member of the Spartanburg, South Carolina, Chamber of Commerce

Colonel Hayward knew that any problems that happened in town would be blamed on his soldiers. "I am depending on you to act like the good soldiers you have always been and break the ice in this country for your entire race," he told them. He made the soldiers pledge to avoid fights, no matter what happened. It was a hard promise to keep. Many stores and restaurants refused to serve the men. Townspeople called them names. Some struck or pushed the soldiers as they walked down the street. A hotel

Colonel William Hayward

manager struck one officer simply because the soldier had not removed his hat when he came inside the hotel.

Then, one day two soldiers were reported missing. A rumor spread that they had been **lynched** in town. Around 40 soldiers went into town to investigate. Colonel Hayward went with them to ensure that everyone remained calm. The missing men turned up the next day. They had simply gotten lost on their way back from town. Yet the concern that the men of the 15th felt was very real. A race riot had broken out in Houston, Texas, after black soldiers were stationed there.

race riot—an outbreak of violence between two or more racial groups
lynch—to be put to death, often by hanging, by mob action and without legal authority

Colonel Hayward feared similar violence would erupt if his troops remained in South Carolina. He asked that the 15th be sent directly to France. After less than two weeks in South Carolina, the regiment traveled to New Jersey. From there they boarded a troop ship bound for Europe. Strong winds rocked the *Pocahontas* as it began its journey on December 13, 1917. The soldiers remained tense throughout the two-week voyage. German submarines prowled the seas. The U-boats, as they were called, attacked military vessels, cargo ships, and even passenger liners. After two weeks, the 15th regiment safely reached France.

The U.S. Army already had two black infantry divisions, the 92nd and 93rd. The 15th regiment was assigned to be part of the 93rd. But the army was still reluctant to let black soldiers fight. Eager to reach the front lines, the 15th had to wait. Like most other African-American troops, they were at first assigned lowly support tasks, such as unloading ships and moving supplies. The men grew discouraged. They wanted to fight the Germans.

African-American soldiers in the segregated U.S. Army during World War I dug trenches for a mass burial.

FINDING ACCEPTANCE

|||||||||||||||||||||||||||||||||||||||||||||||||||||||||||||||

Finally, Hayward appealed directly to General John "Black Jack" Pershing, who headed the U.S. Army forces in France. Pershing had commanded black soldiers in the Spanish-American War in 1898. He knew that black troops could be brave and fight hard. Pershing made it clear that "these regiments were not to be used as labor troops." He offered the regiment to the French army.

After three years of intense fighting, many French soldiers had been killed or wounded. French leaders gratefully accepted Pershing's offer of **reinforcements**. They didn't care what color the soldiers were. They were just happy to have support. Besides, the French did not have the same prejudices against black soldiers as the Americans.

Did You Know?

The men of the 15th were the only American unit to serve under a foreign command during World War I. They wore standard American khaki uniforms but were equipped with blue French steel helmets.

reinforcements—extra troops sent into battle

CHAPTER 4

A FEARED FIGHTING UNIT

Renamed the 369th Infantry Regiment, the men of the 15th trained for a few weeks with the French army. They learned to use French rifles, which worked differently from the ones the U.S. Army used. They also learned the French language so they could understand battle commands.

By early 1918 the Americans had helped turn the tide of the war against the Central Powers. As more American troops arrived, the strength and fighting spirit of the Allied army grew. In March 1918 Germany and Russia signed a treaty. With fighting on the Eastern Front ended, Germany moved hundreds of thousands of soldiers to the Western Front. In the spring and early summer, they launched desperate attacks trying to gain ground and capture Paris. In April 1918 the 369th **deployed** to a position near the Argonne Forest in France. The fighting was taking place not far away.

The soldiers of the 369th lived and fought in trenches just a few hundred feet (about 100 meters) away from the German troops. They faced machine gun fire and grenades. They also endured poison gas attacks. The soldiers put on gas masks to prevent their eyes, skin, and lungs from burning.

deploy—to move troops into position for military action

American troops fought on the front lines in Argonne, France.

DEADLY ADVANCES

Casualties ran higher in World War I than any previous war. One reason was the scale of the fighting. Another was the introduction of deadlier weapons. Rapid-fire machine guns shot faster than rifles. Long-range cannons could shell targets miles away. Meanwhile, airplanes, tanks, and submarines had their first widespread use in battle. The Germans also used flamethrowers. The new weapon shot streams of flame 20 to 30 feet (6 to 9 meters). It could roast soldiers to death in the trenches. Another deadly advance was the use of chemical weapons such as chlorine gas. It burned the eyes and lungs. It caused thousands of deaths until armies began issuing gas masks to protect troops.

SNEAK ATTACKS
||||||||||||||||||||||||||||||||||||||||||||||||

Soldiers in the trenches remained constantly on guard. German soldiers sometimes launched nighttime sneak attacks across the **no-man's land** between the trenches. On May 15 privates Henry Johnson and Needham Roberts became heroes. Serving as guards at the front lines of their trenches, they heard German soldiers cutting through the barbed wire at the edge of no-man's land. They could see little in the cloudy night, but they hurled grenades and fired their rifles at the dark forms coming toward them.

Sergeant Henry Johnson of Albany, New York, proved himself a hero as part of the 369th Regiment.

At one point Johnson saw German soldiers trying to drag Roberts away. He threw himself forward, swinging the heavy battle knife he carried. Finally the Germans fled. Both Johnson and Roberts were badly wounded. But they had killed or wounded more than a dozen Germans and drove them away. Word of their bravery spread.

No Retreat
||||||||||||||||||||||||||||||||||||||

The 369th took pride in the fact that none of its members were ever captured. They also never retreated. In one heated battle, a French officer ordered the 369th to pull back. Hayward replied that his men did not retreat. Then he led his men in a daring charge that forced the Germans to retreat.

"They go forward or they die!"

—Colonel William Hayward on his refusal to allow his troops to retreat

Did You Know?

The Harlem Hellfighters spent 191 days in combat during World War I. This was more than any other U.S. military unit.

no-man's land—the area between enemy trenches where much of the fighting (and dying) took place during World War I

A Fitting Nickname

Many soldiers of the 369th were killed or wounded during the various battles with the Germans. Their German foes admired their bravery. So did their French comrades. Both called the 369th soldiers "hellfighters." The nickname stuck.

> *"Above all the horror of these days of battle, stands out my pride in my men and in their heroism."*
>
> —Captain John Clark speaking about the 369th Regiment after the battle of Meuse-Argonne

In late September 1918 members of the 369th played a key role in the critical Battle of Meuse-Argonne. They captured the key village of Sechault. In that battle they fought their way foot by foot, house by house. Casualties were high. During the three days of fighting, 172 of the regiment's men were killed, and 679 were wounded.

Soon after, Germany asked for peace. A treaty ending the war was signed November 11, 1918. The 369th, along with other black regiments, had played an important role in bringing victory. They had proved that African-American soldiers were just as capable as white soldiers, if not more so.

American troops marched to battle in Argonne, France.

Did You Know?

World War I ranked as the deadliest war ever at the time and the second deadliest in human history. More than 8.5 million soldiers died during World War I. Another 21 million were wounded. Nearly 8 million more were taken prisoner or listed as missing. More than half of the soldiers who took part in the war ended up killed, wounded, taken prisoner, or missing.

CHAPTER 5

RETURNING AS HEROES

The soldiers of the 369th sailed for home in January 1919. They marched proudly to the music of James Europe's band as they boarded ships for home. They marched up Fifth Avenue in New York City as heroes on February 17. Europe's band led the way. Some reports say hundreds of thousands watched the parade. Others say more than a million.

For one day at least, the white community honored the African-American soldiers who had helped the Allies win the war. "The color of their skin had nothing to do with the occasion," reported the *New York Tribune*. "The blood they shed in France was as red as any other."

Soldiers of the U.S. 369th Infantry Regiment were celebrated as heroes in a parade in New York City after the war.

Henry Johnson rode proudly in the back of a car. He was still nursing wounds in both legs that he had received in battle. Many people knew him because of newspaper articles that had been written about him. He drew the loudest cheers as he rode past the crowd. Other wounded soldiers who could not walk rode at the end of the parade.

The celebration grew even more joyous when the parade reached Harlem. A community of mostly blacks, it burst with pride as it greeted the heroes.

A wounded veteran of the U.S. 369th was among those honored at a victory parade in February 1919 in New York City.

African-American schoolchildren had the day off to watch the parade. But in the midst of celebration was a tinge of sadness. The ranks of the 369th had thinned. Roughly half of the unit's men had been killed or wounded in France.

CHAPTER 6

CHANGING THE COURSE OF HISTORY

The Harlem Hellfighters played an important role in helping the Allies win World War I. They also helped change the U.S. military. The 369th and other black fighting regiments in World War I showed great bravery and skill. This helped military leaders realize that blacks could be excellent soldiers. From that time on, the U.S. military became more open to having blacks serve both as soldiers and officers. But it wasn't until after World War II (1939-1945) that the U.S. military was finally desegregated.

Soldiers proudly wore the Croix de Guerre medals they earned for gallantry in action.

Did You Know?

Seventy-one soldiers from the 369th were awarded the Croix de Guerre. The French medal honors bravery in the face of the enemy. Another 21 received the U.S. Distinguished Service Cross. In 2015, more than 80 years after his death and 97 years after the end of the war, Private Henry Johnson was awarded the Medal of Honor.

It took a long time to change the nation's social structure. "It was right of us to fight," wrote W.E.B. Du Bois in 1919. But now, he added, we need to "marshal every ounce of our brain and brawn to fight a sterner, longer, more unbending battle against the forces of hell in our own land."

Once the excitement about the end of the war wore off, many of the men in the 369th continued to face discrimination in their civilian lives. The 369th had fought bravely to defend democracy worldwide. The fight to win equal rights at home took far longer. Race riots shook Chicago and other cities in 1919. In fact, it took 45 years of protests and marches until the Civil Rights Act of 1964 outlawed discrimination based on race, religion, or sex. Even after that, the battle for true equality continues. But the World War I contributions of the 369th helped lay the groundwork for it all.

THE WOUNDED ARTIST

One of the Harlem Hellfighters went on to gain fame in another field after the war. Budding artist Horace Pippin was in no-man's-land on a scouting mission when he was shot in July 1918. The bullet tore through the nerves and muscles in his right arm. For years Pippin could not move his arm. He learned to use his left hand to guide his right arm to create artwork. Over the years he created dozens of paintings and became a famous artist. Many of his paintings showed the horrors of war.

GLOSSARY

abolitionist (ab-uh-LI-shuhn-ist)—a person who supported the banning of slavery

allies (AL-eyes)—people, groups, or countries that work together for a common cause

assassinate (us-SASS-uh-nayt)—to murder a person who is well-known or important

deploy (di-PLOY)—to move troops into position for military action

discrimination (dis-KRI-muh-nay-shuhn) —unfair treatment of a person or group, often because of race, religion, gender, sexual orientation, or age

lynch (LINCH)—to be put to death, often by hanging, by mob action and without legal authority

mobilize (MOH-buh-lyze)—get troops and weapons ready for battle

neutral (NOO-truhl)—not taking sides in a war

no-man's land (NOH-manz LAND)—the area between enemy trenches where much of the fighting (and dying) took place during World War I

prejudice (PREJ-uh-diss)—an opinion about others that is unfair or not based on facts

race riot (RAYSS RYE-uht)—an outbreak of violence between two or more racial groups

reinforcements (ree-in-FORSS-muhnts)— extra troops sent into battle

segregate (SEG-ruh-gayt)—to keep groups of people apart, especially based on race

stereotype (STAYR-ee-oh-tipe)—an overly simple opinion of a person, group, or thing

trench (TRENCH)—a long, narrow ditch dug in the ground to serve as shelter from enemy fire or attack

READ MORE

Lanser, Amanda. *World War I by the Numbers*. America at War by the Numbers. North Mankato, Minn.: Capstone Press, 2016.

Lewis, J. Patrick, and Gary Kelley. *Harlem Hellfighters*. Mankato, Minn.: Creative Editions, 2014.

Myers, Walter Dean, and Bill Miles. *The Harlem Hellfighters: When Pride Met Courage*. New York: Amistad, 2014.

Rasmussen, R. Kent. *World War I for Kids: A History with 21 Activities*. Chicago: Chicago Review Press, 2014.

INTERNET SITES

FactHound offers a safe, fun way to find Internet sites related to this book. All of the sites on FactHound have been researched by our staff.

Here's all you do:
Visit **www.facthound.com**
Type in this code: 9781515733485

Super-cool stuff!

Check out projects, games and lots more at
www.capstonekids.com

CRITICAL THINKING USING THE COMMOM CORE

1. World War I was sometimes called "The War to End All Wars." Why do you think it was called that, and why do you think that prediction turned out to be untrue? (Integration of Knowledge of Ideas)

2. World War I was the deadliest war ever fought at that point in history. What factors made that true? (Key Ideas and Details)

3. How did the war experiences of the 369th differ from those of white regiments? (Craft and Structure)

INDEX